TALL STORIES

COMPILED BY RUSSELL ASH
ILLUSTRATIONS BY MIKE GORDON

AURUM PRESS

First published 1994 by
Aurum Press Limited
25 Bedford Avenue, London WC1B 3AT

Conceived, edited and designed by
Russell Ash & Bernard Higton

A catalogue record of this book is available from
the British Library.

ISBN 1 85410 335 0

10 9 8 7 6 5 4 3 2 1

1998 1997 1996 1995 1994

Printed in Hong Kong by Imago

CONTENTS

CHAPTER 1

HERE IS THE NEWS

RECORD-BREAKERS

In Semarang, Indonesia, Rini Sutomo staged a scorpion sit-in sponsored by the Indonesian Veterans Wives Association, having her entire body covered with live scorpions to raise money for Indonesian Mothers Day.

Rip Powell, a 23-year-old geology student at the University of Southwestern Louisiana, failed half way through his recent attempt to spend 34 hours seated in a tub of ketchup.

Antonio Gonzalez of New York won the 'Biggest Cockroach' contest at Philadelphia Zoo with a two-inch specimen. At a similar contest in New York, several contestants were disqualified when judges discovered that pieces of various cockroaches had been glued together to make larger ones.

Rebecca Archuleta won a new car in a Santa Fe, New Mexico, contest by kissing the car the longest (34 hours, 20 minutes).

Michael Nau won $15,000 from a radio station in Somerville, Alabama, after diving into a pool of cow manure and rotting vegetables in a 'Most Outrageous Stunt' contest.

OOPS...

A 27-year-old man was rushed to hospital in Lincoln, Nebraska, in a critical condition after police found him nude and unconscious beneath a balcony, with four oranges and a partly-eaten apple under him. Police speculated that he fell while trying to juggle with the oranges while naked and eating an apple.

A newspaper advertisement by an organization called New Man Hair was intended to show the before and after effect of their hair replacement technique with a bald man and the same man with a full head of hair. Unfortunately, they managed to get the pictures the wrong way round.

A similar fate befell a British soap powder manufacturer who was attempting to break into the Arab market. A series of posters intended to show how dirty clothes came out brilliantly clean mysteriously resulted in plumetting sales – until someone realized that Arabs read from right to left, and that the posters appeared to show how clean clothes could be made dirty.

In Wilkes-Barre, Pennsylvania, the fire brigade answered an emergency call when Duane Della, aged 14, managed to get his tongue stuck to the wall of his family's freezer.

After Harold Womack, 51, of Phoenix, Arizona, accidentally drove his Porsche 924 into a pit at the Sunset Crater National Monument, he attempted to tow it out by using a 20-ton steamroller he spotted nearby. Womack drove the steamroller over to his car and hopped off to attach a chain. The steamroller kept rolling and flattened the Porsche.

The American Embassy in Bonn prepared an information package to welcome Secretary of State Charles Shultz. Unfortunately, the Secretary of State was George Schultz – Charles is the cartoonist who draws the 'Peanuts' strip.

In DePere, Wisconsin, Kerry Shea, 14, "just lost control" of her toothbrush and swallowed it, but it was retrieved by a doctor.

According to the *Archives of Surgery*, researchers examining medical literature for examples of unusual things people have swallowed found only 31 recorded cases of toothbrush swallowing. Of those, no fewer than four occurred in Durham, North Carolina, in 1986.

An angler on the Rio Negro, a tributary of the Amazon, accidentally struck a tree with his fishing rod. This dislodged a nest of bees, which promptly attacked him, forcing him to leap into the river – whereupon he was eaten by piranhas.

The Florida state campaign to fight illiteracy eventually admitted defeat and abandoned its billboard campaign. Their slogan read, "If you can't read this we can help."

The US Consumer Product Safety Commission was forced to recall 80,000 badges it had distributed to promote toy safety because they were found to be a danger to children. The badges, which read "For kid's sake think toy safety", used a paint with dangerously high lead content, had sharp edges and parts that could be easily swallowed by a child.

Carpenter Lance Grangruth of Duluth, Minnesota, accidentally shot a nail from his nail gun an inch and a half into his head, thereby nailing his hat to his head. "I didn't actually feel it going in," Grangruth reported, adding, "I tried to take my hat off, and it wouldn't come off."

NUDES OF THE WORLD

National Nude Weekend in Dawsonville, Georgia, reached a grand finale in the form of a skydive by eight men wearing nothing but parachutes.

The Gaslights Record Store in Melbourne, Australia, holds an annual 'Nude Day' in which any nude customer wins one free record. Seventy records were given away on the last occasion.

Among the 'approved' student organizations at the University of California at San Diego: the Nude Kite Fliers' Club.

SEASON OF GOODWILL

For the fish who's got everything: fish apartments to fit inside your aquarium, complete with kitchen and living room – only $1,000 from Joey Scaggs of New York City.

Every Christmas for over 30 years Shirley Clarke of De Witt, Iowa, receives the same present from her husband Jerry. Each year he attaches yet another of his toenails to a gold necklace and leaves it in a small box beneath the Christmas tree – and each year she completely ignores it: "My wife thinks it's the most horrible thing she's ever seen," Jerry explains. "She won't have anything to do with it at all." The as-yet unworn necklace was begun as "Just a hare-brained idea. One Christmas when we'd been married about five years I had a rather large toenail and thought, 'Gee, that would be good to put on a gold chain.'"

Any messy eaters in your family? Selfridges' Christmas catalogue offers a £7.95 polka-dot roller blind tie-protector – "Pull it down while you eat that problem bowl of spaghetti, snap it back when you have finished."

ITV's Dickie Davies will have Irish eyes shining next Wednesday when he turns day into night. The World of Sport link-man was asked by the council at Bangor, Co. Down to switch on their Christmas lights. Dickie couldn't make the evening switch-on. "No problem", said the council. "Do it at lunchtime." (*The Sun*)

Police in Superior, Wisconsin, arrested Richard E. Roehm, 54, for disorderly conduct after he annoyed patrons in the Casablanca Bar with excessive Santa Claus imitations. A bar employee said Roehm was calling people his elves, "Ho-ho-ho-ing and so on." He said he couldn't leave the bar because he was waiting for his sleigh and reindeer.

IT'S A MIRACLE!

Danny Davis, an evangelist from Bakersfield, California, promotes himself as 'God's Dentist' because, when he preaches, members of his congregations are alleged to find gold and silver fillings appearing in their teeth.

At Selma High School, Selma, Alabama, a visiting New York church group performing a passion play was thrown into disarray when the actor playing Jesus refused to get on the cross, claiming it was not sturdy enough. A fight ensued, and when the curtain opened for the final scene the audience was baffled to see Judas on the cross, while the actor playing Jesus sulked in his dressing room.

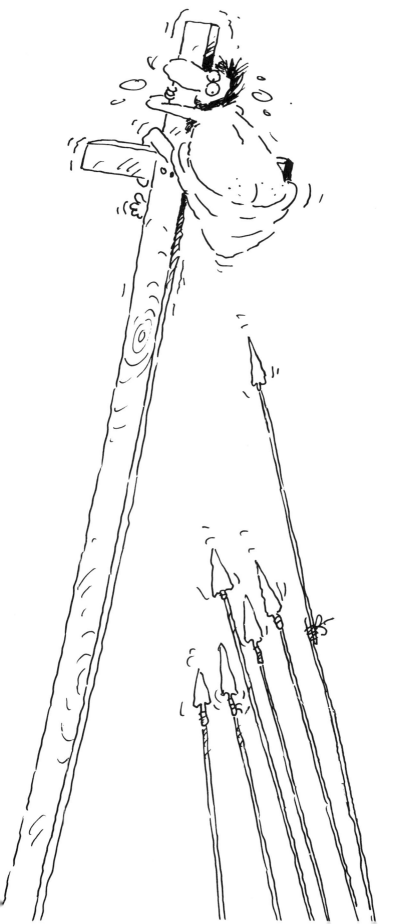

NAME CHANGES

A De Kalb County, Georgia, Superior Court ruled that Gary Eugene Duda, 35, could change his first name to 'Zippidy'. Duda said that he had already been called 'Zippidy' by friends for most of his life.

Following a dispute with the Taxation Department, a resident of Adelaide, Australia, changed his name to 'Mr Screw the Taxpayer to Support Big Government and its Parasites'.

A Colorado man won $10,000 in a radio contest the aim of which was for contestants to change their names to that of the station. The winner produced 53 legal documents proving that he was now called 'Mr The New Q103 FM'.

The US Board on Geographic Names has 'cleaned up' a number of American placenames, including Whorehouse Meadow, Oregon, which is now called Naughty Girl Meadow, and Nellie's Nipple, a mountain in Arizona, which has become College Peak.

KIDS' STUFF

Police in Seattle, Washington, took three brothers aged seven, eight and nine into custody after they set off a fire alarm. While they attempted to locate their parents the boys caused mayhem in the police station by yelling and screaming, brandishing and stabbing each other and police officers with plastic knives, covering themselves and a squad car with chewing gum, locking themselves in a lavatory where they wrote on the walls, swinging billiard cues and hurling billiard balls round the officers' lounge, banging on cell doors and throwing objects at windows in an attempt to break out. When their father eventually arrived, he admitted he had been having trouble with the boys lately.

Hal Warden, 16, of Nashville, Tennessee, divorced his wife Catherine, 13. He had previously been married at the age of 12 to an older woman, Wendy Chappel, 14. Wendy won custody of their child by telling the judge that Hal was "Acting like a 10-year-old."

In Grosse Pointe Woods, Michigan, a 15-year-old boy pulled a gun on his dentist and forced him to remove his tooth braces, declaring that jail was preferable to continuing to wear the braces.

Within two months a two-year-old girl, Robin Hawkins of Grand Rapids, Michigan, has destroyed her family's television, dishwasher and refrigerator, flushed the cat down the toilet and managed to start their car, causing it to crash into a tree and resulting in over $1,000-worth of damages. Among her other numerous acts of mayhem are painting the walls with nail polish and drilling 50 holes in them, slipping a tractor out of gear so it narrowly missed a neighbour and filching $620 out of a supermarket cash register.

SCHOOL REPORTS

University of Miami microbiologist Patricia Mertz sought volunteers with smelly feet so that she could test her theory that the odour was similar to that of Limburger cheese. Her researchers planned to sniff cheese to familiarize themselves with the scent, then study five volunteers a day for 48 days, at a distance of two inches.

Students at West Delaware High School, Manchester, Iowa, who go to the toilet during classes are required by some teachers to wear toilet seats round their necks or to carry rolls of toilet paper. The policy is designed to cut down on the number of toilet requests by students.

Boy Scouts in Media, Pennsylvania, postponed their January 'winter survival' skills training until June as a result of inclement weather.

Sherry McDonald, an Indianapolis substitute teacher, was suspended for arranging for the well-behaved children in her class to line up and spit on the bad ones.

KIDS: DON'T TRY THIS AT HOME

The Morbidity and Mortality Weekly Report, published by the Centers for Disease Control, has issued stern warnings against the following dangerous activities: eating raw pork intestines, poking one's eye with a mascara brush, entering unventilated manure pits and exposure to rabid llamas.

Mabel Wolf, an assistant in a Brooklyn hardware shop, often entertained her colleagues by eating nails and other metal objects. When she was operated on, a surgeon removed 1,203 items. Mabel explained, "I guess I did it to be funny."

Two men and a woman in a bar in Austin, Nevada, had to have rabies injections after one of the men found a dead rabid bat and, as a joke, dunked it into their beer.

TODAY'S BIG STORIES

At Columbus, Ohio, the trial of 43-stone Daniel M. Elkins had to be conducted in the court hall because he was too big to get through the door. On finding him guilty, the court paid a piano-moving company $75 to carry him to prison.

Tifton, Georgia, prosecutors arranged a makeshift witness stand to hear testimony about stolen goods from pawnshop owner Sylvanus 'Hambone' Smith. Since Smith weighed 900 pounds (more than 64 stone) and could not move more than eight steps without resting, he was transported to the front of the courthouse on a truck, with the jury listening from the lobby, because he couldn't fit into the witness stand.

Stanley Walker, 47, was killed in a domestic dispute with his wife, Vannie, in Bridgeport, Connecticut. When he called her a "Fat-assed ox" and threatened to burn their house down, Vannie, who weighs 36 stone, sat on him and squashed him to death.

A women's weight-loss class in Penzance was cancelled when a local official complained that the combined weight of the class (over three tons) "seriously overstressed" the building.

Earlean Davis, 47, was jailed in Houston, Texas, for 10 years on shoplifting charges. Described as "rather large", she had been caught attempting to walk out of shops with fox fur and mink coats and a television set between her legs. Assistant District Attorney Dan Smythe told the court that when Ms Davis bent over to pick something up, employees of the shop noticed the shape of a large $695-television under her dress.

In Prague, a 36-stone 52-year-old man identified only as 'Zbynek M.' was jailed for 12 years for stealing £75,000-worth of food.

WHY, OH WHY?

Creighton Miller, 22, of Altadena, California, chopped off his own left foot because he believed he had sinned against God by treading on some insects.

When Clint Bolin vacated his Long Beach, California apartment, the landlord found he had left 600 boxes containing 30 tons of rocks stacked to the ceiling in every room. Bolin's behaviour was never explained, but it was discovered that he had left similar piles of rock-filled boxes in motel rooms he had stayed in, sometimes only overnight.

In the Maricopa County Recorder's Office, Richard Gary Griffing of Mesa, Arizona, filed a claim on the planet Mars, advising the US Government that he will allow American spacecraft to land there without charge, but intends banning unsolicited telephone calls and mobile homes from 'his' planet.

In Knoxville, Illinois, the widow and two children of Carl Stevens were found to have been looking after him as though he were ill, when in fact he had been dead for eight years. Sheriff Mark Shearer explained, "Let's just say the family has abnormal beliefs in the power of healing."

SPORTS REPORTS

At the recently-opened Talamore golf course in Pinehurst, North Carolina, golfers can choose between renting a golf cart to transport their clubs – or a llama.

LADIES SHOWERS

Erika Schinegger of Austria returned his 1966 women's world ski championship medal, confessing that in 1968 he had discovered he was a man.

For its Australian rules football match against Lunceston Reserves, Tasmanian football team Longford Reserves managed to field only 16 instead of the 19 players required, and these were all schoolboys, injured or retired players. By half time, finding themselves losing 210 points to nil, they sent a message to their opponents, "Blow this for a lark. We give up." And they all went home.

In Gorizia, Italy, an undercover policeman foiled a plot to slip powerful laxatives into World champion Giuseppe Saroni's food to prevent him from winning an Italian cycle race.

The Zimbabwe Football Association banned four soccer players for life for urinating on the field in Harare because witch doctors told them it would ensure victory. They lost as well, 2–nil.

A court in Versailles, France, overturned an order banning dwarf-tossing, thus permitting 3-foot 11-inch Manuel Wackenheim, 24, to return to his job at the Eclipse nightclub in Morsang-sur-Orge, where he had been prevented from working as a result of the ban. A French Government Minister had called such shows "an intolerable attack on human dignity," but the Government finally conceded that such a prohibition would deny a 'physically different' (or, in politically correct jargon, 'vertically challenged') person a chance of a livelihood.

YOU COULD SEE IT COMING

Channel 5 in Nashville, Tennessee, held a 'Mission: Bermuda Triangle' contest, offering viewers a chance to win a seven-day holiday in Florida. The competition had to be re-started after all the entries mysteriously disappeared.

Penny Pellito, 52, of Miramar, Florida, a housewife and psychic, sued a shop where a plank fell on her head, causing her to lose many of her powers – although she says she can still pick winning racehorses. She explained that she never claimed to have the power to anticipate falling objects in shops.

In a dwarf-tossing contest, an old record of seven feet nine inches was beaten by two competitors, who managed to throw the dwarf, David Wilson, a full nine feet. Despite complaints by residents that the event was demeaning to dwarves, Wilson drew loud cheers when he swore repeatedly that he was having a good time.

BUSINESS NEWS

Animalens of Wellesley, Massachusetts, sells red contact lenses for chickens at 20 cents a pair. They claim that research has shown that chickens that see red during the day are happier, eat less food and lay more eggs. (Spectacle-wearing chickens are nothing new, incidentally: in 1903 Andrew Jackson Jr. of Munich, Tennessee, patented hen goggles to prevent chickens from pecking each other's eyes.)

A weekly Soviet magazine criticized an incompetent Ukrainian shoe factory that had issued a shipment of boots with high heels attached to the toes.

David Kendrick of Berkshire, New York, has patented a watch that runs in reverse chronological order. The wearer sets his life expectancy according to an actuarial table, and the watch indicates how much time he has left on Earth. Kendrick says the watch will encourage people not to waste time.

• •

GOVERNMENT IN ACTION

Members of the Georgia State Game Commission seriously debated the merits of regulating alligator rides for some time before one of the commissioners realized that the agenda contained a typing error and they were supposed to be discussing alligator *hides*.

The former Governor of South Dakota, William Janklow, once admitted that he sometimes relaxed in his mansion wearing bunny pyjamas with built-in tail and rabbit feet.

The fireman's club at Penistone, Yorkshire, was closed down when it was declared a fire hazard.

LOST PROPERTY

While passengers of London Transport have managed to lose such items as a stuffed gorilla and an outboard motor, they have a long way to go to compete with forgetful Japanese passengers who in a single year managed to leave on trains 500,000 umbrellas, £10 million in cash, 29 small dogs, one live snake in a bag, 150 sets of false teeth and 15 urns containing ashes of the dead.

Workers draining the lake under a roller coaster at Blackpool found hundreds of pairs of false teeth, several wigs and six glass eyes – all presumably shaken loose during the ride.

—— CHAPTER 2 ——

FOOD FOR THOUGHT

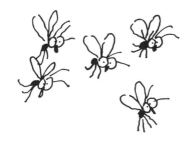

GRUB-U-LIKE

Oregon State University entomologist Michael Burgett (whose own favourites are head lice and fly pupae) has calculated that the average American unwittingly eats about a pound of insects and other small creatures every year. They are left in many food products since the removal of portions of them would be prohibitively expensive. (In fact, such ingredients are quite permissible: the Public Health Service of the United States Food and Drug Administration publishes 'defect levels' which are not to be exceeded in foodstuffs. A 100 gram bar of chocolate may thus legally contain up to 60 microscopic insect fragments and an average of 1.5 rodent hairs.)

As long ago as 1885, Vincent Holt, author of an extraordinary treatise, *Why Not Eat Insects?*, attempted to overcome our prejudices against eating unconventional foodstuffs, suggesting such unusual dishes as Moth on Toast. One of his mouthwatering menus offered:

Starter:
Slug Soup
Boiled Cod with Snail Sauce

Main course:
Wasp Grubs fried in the Comb
Moths sautéed in Butter
Braised Beef with Caterpillars
New Carrots with Wireworm Sauce

Dessert:
Gooseberry Cream with Sawflies
Devilled Chafer Grubs
Stag Beetle Larvae on Toast

SPAM, SPAM, SPAM

At Rhode Island College's first Spam Art Festival, the winning entry was Spamhenge, a model of the historic ruin made completely from Spam.

Mark Carey, 27, won the 16th Annual Spamput Championship in Austin, Texas, by tossing the contents of a can of Spam 60 feet. Other events included the Spam-Cram, in which contestants had to force 12 ounces of Spam into their mouths and swallow it all, and the Spam-Calling Contest (related to Hog-Calling, in which pigs are summoned by their owner using a sing-song call – the principal difference with Spam being that the pig is dead, and in a can). It was won by Dr Bud Luecke with a memorable call that ranged from rumbling to whining "Spammy Spammy Spammy Spammy".

DEADLY MEALS

A Parisian nightwatchman apparently killed his second wife because she overcooked a roast. Seventeen years earlier, he had killed his first wife because she had undercooked a meal.

Annette Williams of Washington, DC, was charged with murdering her sister for preparing too many potatoes in a meal.

Carl Trice of Chicago stabbed his brother to death after discovering him defrosting a pork chop he had bought for himself.

Daniel Lopez of Carlsbad, New Mexico, was arrested for shooting his live-in girlfriend. "Wouldn't you be mad," he asked, "if all you had to eat was green beans all the time?"

Lawrence Timmons was killed by the chef in a Whataburger restaurant in an incident that arose after Timmons had become aggressive on learning that the restaurant had run out of large buns.

A Norfolk, Virginia, McDonald's manager was killed because he refused to refund money for an unsatisfactory cheeseburger.

THE GOOD LOO GUIDE

Even though the restaurant seats only 18, local officials insisted that the Corner Deli in Collinsville, Illinois, should build a second toilet. In response the owners, Ed and Sandy Dawdy, installed one in their front window.

From Toto Ltd of Japan comes the Sound Princess, a gadget the only function of which is to emit the sound of flushing water. Many Japanese people are so embarrassed about using the lavatory that they flush it repeatedly to cover the sound of their activity, wasting millions of gallons of water.

Gordon and Jasmine Geisbrecht opened a restaurant called 'The Outhouse' in a suburb of Winnipeg, Canada. Built on the theme of toilets, toilet bowls were placed among the tables, and a toilet seat logo appeared on the menus. Health inspectors soon forced the restaurant to suspend operations – because it lacked adequate lavatories.

CHAPTER 3

CRIMINAL ACTIVITIES

In Manila, a man stabbed and killed his brother and wounded a friend during an argument over whether Imelda Marcos was prettier than Princess Diana.

Car thieves in Changwa, Taiwan, have taken to leaving ransom notes and homing pigeons at the spot from which they have stolen cars. They then wait at their hideouts for the pigeons to arrive with the ransom money. Police have so far been unable to follow the pigeons.

California Highway Patrol officer Dave Guild stopped a car travelling 50 mph on the San Diego Freeway because its bonnet was open and a man was under it working on the engine. The driver and mechanic said that they had been having trouble with the accelerator and the man under the bonnet was keeping the engine running by operating the carburettor control. Neither could understand why they were being booked.

Police in Santa Monica, California, arrested a 48-year-old man whose real name is Jesus Christ. He was charged with driving under the influence of alcohol.

An 18-year-old man was sentenced to 10 years in prison in Jacksonville, Florida, on a charge of drug-related murder. He explained that he had been driven into a life of crime because, he claimed, "People expected me to live up to my namesake." His father said he had named him Adolph Hitler Clark "Because he was famous."

Nathan Hicks of St Louis shot and killed his brother Herbert with a rifle because Herbert had used six of the eight rolls of toilet paper Nathan had bought two days earlier.

EXCUSES, EXCUSES, EXCUSES...

A New York boat mechanic was convicted of the murder of a Long Island man and sentenced to life imprisonment. The jury did not accept his explanation that he stabbed his victim seventy-two times and ran over him with a car in self-defence.

A man accused of indecent exposure in a car park in Gastonia, New Mexico, was found not guilty after claiming that a bee had flown into his trousers and that he had removed them to swat it.

A jury in Reading, Pennsylvania, was unconvinced by the explanation of Henry Deblec that he had been growing marijuana to cure his piles.

COMPLETELY QUACKERS

An unidentified 40-year-old man was arrested in San Antonio after causing a commotion at a local bank. According to a bank spokesperson, when the man was told his loan application had not been approved, he stripped naked and began to quack like a duck. When police arrived he answered their questions by quacking and then caused $1,000-worth of damage to a squad car by kicking it.

A man robbed Wayne's Bait and Supply in Osage Beach, Missouri, and to prevent the owner, his wife, his daughter and a customer from chasing him, glued them to the floor with Super Glue.

LUCKY ESCAPE

In Hialeah, Florida, Federal Drug Agent Carlos Montalvo's life was saved when a bullet he fired lodged in the barrel of a suspect's own drawn gun.

LEFT SPEECHLESS

After the two finalists had gabbled their way to a total of 91 hours in a talking contest in Melbourne, they learned that the contest organizers had vanished with the prize money.

BIG ROBBERY

A three-bedroom house was reported stolen from Neaves Road, Waneroo, a suburb of Perth, Australia. Ray Marinko returned from holiday to find his home had disappeared. Police issued a description: "White, with kitchen, dining room, lounge, bathroom and interior toilet. Anyone seeing a building answering this description should contact their local police station."

LITTLE-KNOWN LAWS

A law still on the books in Pocatello, Idaho, makes it illegal to "Frown, grimace or scowl" or to "Have any facial expression that reflects unfavourably on Pocatello."

Anyone detonating a nuclear weapon within the city limits of Chico, California, is liable to a $500 fine.

Councillors in Richmond, Virginia, passed a motion proposing that dead bodies should be kept out of places where food is served.

In London, under Section 23 of the Royal and Other Parks and Gardens Regulations of 1977, "touching a pelican" is forbidden in London's parks – unless written permission is first obtained.

New legislation passed by the Arkansas General Assembly makes it illegal to extract the teeth or otherwise "surgically alter" a bear.

Republican Will Green Poindexter backed a bill in Mississippi to permit dwarfs to hunt deer with crossbows.

Wyoming legislature recently banned the photographing of rabbits during January, February, March and April without an official permit.

Robert Haag was charged with attempting to steal a 37-ton meteorite (roughly the size of a car) from Chaco province, Argentina, in order to smuggle it out of the country.

As an armed robber held up a restaurant in Arlington, Virginia, demanding "Stick 'em up!" a waiter threw up his hands, splattering the gunman with tomato ketchup from the bottle he was holding. The robber wiped his face, saw his 'bloodstained' fingers and, thinking he had been wounded, immediately surrendered.

Al Hargis, 28, told police who arrested him after discovering him spinning round in a clothes dryer in a New Hampshire laundrette, "I wanted to see what it was like riding in a space ship."

PIPE OF PEACE

An Indian, Myron Everett Warrior, aged 21, from South Dakota, was sentenced to six months imprisonment for assaulting another Indian, Bruce Pipe On Head, by hitting him on the head, with a pipe.

SILLY BEES

Nairobi police arrested a Greek nun known as 'Sister Irene' and charged her with smuggling 6,000 bees into Kenya under her habit. She told the Kenya Times that she wanted the beeswax to make candles. (The importation of bee paraphernalia into various parts of Africa is strictly controlled – it is, for example, illegal to post secondhand bee-keeping equipment to Botswana – so do be careful what you put in the post.)

NO WAY TO TREAT A DOGG

James Dogg, 42, was charged with assault in Mandan, North Dakota, for beating up his girl-friend's mother, 86-year-old Regina Lafromboise, who had been taunting Dogg about his name and repeatedly making barking noises.

DON'T MESS WITH THIS WOMAN

In Canada Nicole Laurin was charged with hiring a hitman to murder Remi Nahai, 20, because she was fed up with his Pontiac, minus silencer, thundering past her home. She was also suspected of poisoning her husband after he had threatened to turn her in for hiring the hitman.

BATMAN & ROBBER

At Halloween in Tallahassee, Florida, K-Mart employee Jeff Sablom was trying on the Batman costume he planned to wear that evening when a security guard asked him to help arrest a shoplifter who was stealing cigarettes and videotapes. The guard said later, "You should have seen that man's eyes when he looked back and saw Batman chasing him!"

GREAT ESCAPES

Jack Kelm was caught by police as he fled after a bank robbery in Boulder, Colorado, on a bicycle. Mr Kelm is 82 years old.

In New Haven, Connecticut, William McNellis, 43, was caught after an attempted bank robbery that failed when the getaway car he left idling outside was stolen. He was sentenced to eighty years in prison.

Rory Johnson, 29, was arrested after a liquor store robbery in Elkhart, Indiana. He had parked behind the store to make a quick getaway, but when he attempted to drive away got caught in a traffic jam. Five minutes after the robbery, he was still sitting in his car, having moved only a few feet, while employees of the store he had robbed pointed him out to the police.

In Colorado a man was arrested and handcuffed behind his back for drunk driving, but when the officer left him unattended he was amazed to see his police car disappear at high speed. The resultant chase, at speeds up to 105 mph, went on for sixty miles before the police could re-arrest the drunk – who was steering with his teeth.

COP FLOPS

Errors in the system used by Paris police in coding offences recently led to 41,000 people being misclassified: those with traffic tickets were accused of manslaughter, people charged with murder were ordered to pay small fines and those who had driven through red lights were listed as having illegally imported veterinary medicines.

Psychology professor Robert A. Baron has advised Cincinnati police to use novel techniques to defuse violent domestic disputes. When they arrive at the scene, he recommends that they should try performing Bugs Bunny impressions, pretend to raid the refrigerator or pull their hats down to make their ears stick out, so as to "disarm the combatants with humour."

From a report on multiple murders in Washington: A police spokesman said the bodies were discovered about 4.40 pm on Wednesday. "We're working on the theory that whatever happened occurred before that," the spokesman said.

In Gainesville, Florida, police staked out a motorcycle for 17 days in the hope of catching an elusive bike thief. He struck again when the officer on duty took two minutes off to use the toilet.

Police in Crown Point, Indiana, treated the death of James A. Cooley, 52, as a suicide for several weeks until public pressure forced a reopening of the case and its re-classification as a murder. Police acknowledged all along that Cooley had died as a result of 32 hammer blows to the head.

In Van Nuys, California, the police allowed Dennis John Alston, who had been arrested for forgery, to be bailed with an exact copy of the forged $1,500 cheque that had resulted in his arrest.

"DROP THAT HAMBURGER!"

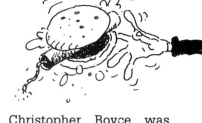

—AND OTHER DEADLY WEAPONS

When counterspy Christopher Boyce was arrested by US agents in a fast-food restaurant in Seattle, the officer in charge demanded, "Drop that hamburger!"

As she left an ice-cream parlour, a 52-year-old woman in Albany, New York, was confronted by a man who demanded her purse. According to police spokesman Sgt Robert Wolfgang, "She repeatedly struck him with a hot-fudge sundae she was carrying," as a result of which he fled empty-handed.

Donald Morris Smith was sentenced to 70 years imprisonment in Tarboro, North Carolina, after beating the owner of a sweet factory to death with a 30-inch long 9-pound stick of rock.

In 1978 a Paris grocer stabbed his wife to death with a wedge of Parmesan cheese.

In Flushing, New York, Milton Eberenz, 74, was charged with the manslaughter of his 69-year-old companion, Jean Benes, by pushing her into a folding bed.

Police in Wisconsin Rapids, Wisconsin, investigating the death of 30-year-old Mary Herman, ascertained that she was killed by a "crushing type injury" as though a car had run over her but mysteriously left no tyre marks. They concluded that an elephant was the fatal weapon and later charged two animal trainers from a circus that had passed through the town.

Barney Cobb of Birmingham, Alabama, was convicted for assault after repeatedly beating his wife over the head with their pet chihuahua.

THICK AS THIEVES

Using a toy gun, Paul Bernier attempted to rob the Lafayette Cooperative Bank in Swansea, Massachusetts. He fainted during the robbery and was arrested, but according to police he would not have escaped anyway, having locked his keys in the getaway car.

A middle-aged woman in Lausanne, Switzerland, fainted in a supermarket and medical assistance was summoned. A nurse who decided to ease the

woman's breathing by unhooking her bra discovered a shoplifted frozen chicken inside, and concluded that the woman had fainted from the cold.

Los Angeles police arrested James Richardson, 32, and Jeffrey Defalco, 18, for stealing a 3-ton safe that had been left on a pavement while contractors waited for a forklift truck to move it. Their modus operandi was to tow it away behind their car, but the deafening noise and showers of sparks it created as they dragged it along soon alerted police, who simply followed the gouges in the road until they caught up with the pair. The safe was empty anyway.

Baltimore police arrested Thomas Waddell for stealing 30 valuable homing pigeons. He was spotted by a police officer proceeding down the street, but walking oddly because he had 21 of the birds stuffed into his clothing. According to the policeman, "He looked like the Michelin tyre ad."

Police in Arlington, Texas, were greatly assisted in solving an armoured-car robbery. The robber, with gun in hand running for his car, was parked beside a busload of Japanese tourists, who aimed their cameras when they heard the commotion. When their films were developed, many prints showing the man's face and car number plate became available, and he was picked up soon afterwards.

Eugene 'Butch' Flenough Jr of Austin, Texas was sought after an armed robbery at a pizza restaurant. As a disguise, he had worn a crash helmet with 'Butch' and 'Eugene Flenough Jr' printed on it.

In Pittsburgh, Pennsylvania, Elwood Nolden, 34, robbed a bank but left behind the note demanding money. It was written on the back of a letter addressed to him and ordering him to appear in court on another charge.

Thomas Lee Jones, 24, was arrested for robbing a Santa Barbara, California, restaurant with a note threatening "to shot" (sic) employees. Police immediately set up a road block, asked motorists to spell "shoot" and quickly arrested Jones.

Near Cartersville, Georgia, a man received second and third degree burns when he attempted to steal the copper wiring from a live 46,000-volt power line.

A 22-year-old man was arrested in Hutchinson, Kansas, after stealing a large wheeled arc-welder. Police simply followed the tyre tracks from where it was stolen to the thief's garage.

A six-foot-three man tried to rob the same bank in Arlington, Virginia, twice in a four hour period. On both occasions the teller placed the money in a bag, along with an exploding dye pack that coats the money with a coloured dust. Both times the dye exploded just outside the bank, scaring the robber, and both times he fled empty handed.

Suspected purse-snatcher Dereese Delon Waddell stood in a police identity parade so that a 76-year-old woman victim could see him. When police told him to put his baseball cap on with the peak facing forwards, he protested: "No – I'm going to put it on backwards. That's the way I had it on when I took the purse!"

In Deridder, Louisiana, J. Douglas Cresswell, 51, was sentenced to 25 years in prison for three robberies, the last of which went dramatically wrong. Having failed to cut eye-holes in the plastic rubbish bag he wore over his head, his getaway from the bank was foiled as he flailed helplessly inside the bag.

Brendan Maloney aroused suspicion when he tried to cash a Giro cheque in the name of Abdul Khaliq. He spoke in a broad Irish accent, Miss Francois Snape, prosecuting, told Birmingham magistrates. She said Post Office staff asked for identification and he returned with his Irish birth certificate on which his name had been crossed out and replaced by that of Abdul Khaliq. Maloney, of no fixed address, admitted receiving the Giro, worth £49.25, and attempting to use it by deception. He was fined £100 with an alternative of one day in jail.

Patrick M. O'Connor, 21, was arrested after an attempted grocery-store robbery in Calgary, Canada. He was hampered by two things: his only weapon was an ordinary can opener, which did not scare the shop assistant, and he was accompanied during the robbery by his girlfriend's 16-month-old baby, who kept falling out of its pushchair while O'Connor made his getaway.

In Taormina, Italy, a bank robber was caught when, two weeks after his crime, he returned to the same bank to open a savings account.

A man suspected of robbing a jeweller's in Liège, Belgium, claimed he could not have done it because he was busy breaking into a school at the time. Police then arrested him for breaking into the school.

Facing a charge of being involved in an armed robbery at a Liverpool nightclub, Carl McIntyre of Elm Road, Liverpool, denied the charge because he said he was carrying out a burglary at a betting shop at the time.

Pleading 'not guilty' to robbing a female Texaco garage cashier, Jeffrey Johnson opted to conduct his own defence. When a detective he was cross-examining referred to the woman as a "witness", Johnson responded, "What are you talking about some witness, man? There was only me and her in the store."

An Oklahoma jury took just 20 minutes to convict a man of armed robbery. In court, the victim of the robbery identified him as his assailant, at which point the defendant leapt up and accused him of lying. "I should have blown your ****ing head off," he said, quickly adding, "If I'd been the one that was there…"

John J. Cotle was sentenced to six and a half years in prison for burglary in Allentown, Pennsylvania. The main evidence against him was the photographs he took of himself, posing with the stolen goods within hours of the burglary, and which police found in his apartment.

Kevin E. Tibbs was arrested in Brunswick, Maryland. According to police officer Robin Purdum, Tibbs had attempted to steal a parking meter and was trying to conceal it down his trousers when he was apprehended.

In Harrieta, Michigan, Gregory Danford entered a Methodist church on Sunday morning and held the congregation hostage with a rifle. While police were on their way to the scene, a parishioner asked Danford how much the gun cost. When Danford said $500, another parishioner offered him the same price for it, which he accepted. The hostages then took up a collection for the money, Danford handed the rifle over, and the police arrested him.

John Campbell was charged with shoplifting in Seekonk, Massachusetts, after attempting to smuggle a seven-pound live lobster past a supermarket cashier.

YOU BE THE JUDGE

A West German court rejected an £18,000 claim against a group of cleaners at a Dusseldorf art gallery who had allegedly destroyed a valuable sculpture. The judge ruled that the exhibit, a five-pound lump of rancid butter, was not art.

When 21-stone David Todd Brown was sentenced to two years in jail in Santa Clara County, California, on burglary charges, he dropped his trousers and 'mooned' judge Joseph Biafore. The judge promptly added six months to his sentence.

A judge in Howard County, Maryland, revoked the liquor licence of the Boots 'n' Saddles Bar for violating regulations relating to serving drinks to 'impaired' customers. An undercover policeman observed that customers who had passed out were revived by barmaids so that they could buy another drink.

San Francisco police lieutenant George La Brash claimed $18,000 in disability pay after suffering a stroke during a King Tutankhamen exhibition in 1979, which he believed was caused by the Curse of King Tut.

A man who drove his car down the wrong side of a highway in Pontiac, Michigan, and struck another car head-on, killing Sigmund and Irene Fitz, sued for damages from their estate. He told a jury his life had fallen apart since the 1976 accident and that he often felt he would be better off dead. His lawyer added that his client was entitled to damages because the driver of the other car was partially at fault for not swerving out of his way before the collision.

Over a 30-year period, Bea Miles of Sydney's belief that taxi rides should be free of charge landed her in court no fewer than 195 times for evading fares.

A Nairobi rock 'n' roll band called Kerage Success was sued by a Kenyan woman for defamation in a song which, she claimed, likened her "To a hen with no fixed address."

JAIL NEWS

A new 195-cell jail being built for Duval County, Florida, had no doors because none were included in the original plans. Director of Jails Michael Berg said he wasn't sure how it happened, but that it would cost $1.5 million to put right.

In order to save $600,000 in building a San Diego jail, the authorities had ordered walls made of plasterboard and polystyrene instead of concrete, making the construction weaker than the local dog

Warden Jerry Gilmore of the Henry C. Hill Correctional Center in Galesbury, Illinois, was criticized for spending $180 of his budget on six skateboards for inmates' use.

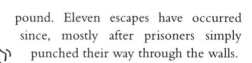

pound. Eleven escapes have occurred since, mostly after prisoners simply punched their way through the walls.

During a warden's strike, as a prank, inmates in a prison in New South Wales, Australia, broke into an office and telephoned an order for 18 tons of concrete to be delivered to the jail. They also ordered 312 pizzas. The concrete was later sent back, but the pizzas were delivered and the prison had to pay for them.

Despite being handcuffed and in leg irons, Henry Leroy Hensen skipped away from Patton State Mental Hospital in San Bernardino County, California – using a skipping rope. His lawyer explained to the judge that Hensen made the rope at a hospital macramé class.

In Cranston, Rhode Island, Donald M. Thomas escaped from jail after serving 89 days of a 90-day sentence for disorderly conduct – as a result of which he faced up to 20 years in prison for escaping.

CHAPTER 4

BEASTLY BEHAVIOUR

MONKEY BUSINESS

Under a new law, owners of monkeys in Indonesia must obtain an identity card for the animal – complete with a photo of the monkey.

An article in *The Lancet* describing a spinal defect that causes sufferers to slouch like apes was illustrated with side-by-side photographs of a human victim and an ape. To disguise the identity of the human, there was a black square over his face – but there was also one over the ape's.

Congo, a pet chimpanzee, raided the drinks cabinet while his owner, Mario Cervantes of Hollis, Queens, New York, was out and guzzled down a quart of vodka and two bottles of beer. He then crashed through the window and out into the street where he went on a drunken rampage, breaking windows and biting a neighbour's toe, until Mr Cervantes appeared and persuaded Congo to return home.

FLATTENED FAUNA

After her cat, Felix, was run over by an 18-wheel truck, Mrs Oramae Lewis of Bedford, Ohio, handed his squashed body to veterinarian Marshall Pettibone who had him freeze-dried by a machine normally used to freeze-dry coffee. Mrs Lewis was delighted with the result, commenting, "He's just like he was in real life – except he's a little flatter in the middle."

Elaine Houghland, 20, entered a contest organized by Louisville radio station WDXJ to find the most creative use of its name. She submitted nine dead animals – squirrels, cats, opossums and a chicken – wired to a board in the shape of 'WDXJ'. Houghland claimed that she had scraped them off the road, but a local animal agency spokesman alleged that she had killed them deliberately to enter the contest.

Ms Houghland would probably be interested in Roger M. Knutson's book, Flattened Fauna: A Field

Guide to Common Animals of Roads, Streets and Highways, which is, states the author, "devoted to making the experience of seeing dead animals on the road meaningful, even enjoyable."

ANIMAL LOVERS

A 32-year-old man in Woodbury, New Jersey, pleaded guilty to aggravated assault and animal cruelty after an argument with his girlfriend during which he attempted to stuff pieces of Abraham, her pet iguana, down her throat.

Shaun Desborough was fined £200 in Hull after biting a dog.

Fearful of being embarrassed in front of royal visitors at a mynah bird speaking contest in Lamut, Malaysia, the organizers set up a pre-contest censorship audition to disqualify swearing birds.

THIS LITTLE PIGGY...

In western Kenya 13 stray pigs broke into drums of an illegal local brew called kangara and drank so much of it that they passed out. When they came to, they went on a wild rampage through the town of Eldoret, terrorizing children and damaging several homes.

During a music festival the Orlando, Florida, branch of the American Society for the Prevention of Cruelty to Animals successfully prevented a display of pig sky-diving.

After a three-year study, the Pig Research Council announced in Canberra, Australia, that slapping pigs raises their blood pressure and reduces their fertility.

DE, DI DE.

DOG-GONE

Robert Beckley left his dog inside his car while he played golf in Durango, New Mexico. The dog knocked the car out of gear, sending it over a cliff and completely wrecking it. The dog escaped alive and was last seen running down the road.

A treadmill for dogs, 'Jog-a-Dog', is on the market in the USA, to enable dogs to run on the spot in the privacy of their own homes.

When Joseph Vellone, of Norwalk, Connecticut, opened his car door at a red light to spit, Ebony, his eight-month-old Alsatian, pushed him out. She then sat in the front seat alone while the car rolled through a junction and crashed into a building.

Clifford Edwards of Merrit Island, Florida, married his dog, Spunky, in a ceremony attended by 100 guests.

A resident of Oak Harbor, Washington, reported his neighbour for putting his dog on the bonnet of his car and driving along at 70 mph. The indignant owner declared that the dog loved it.

Michael E. Brownridge, 28, was arrested in St Louis and charged with stealing about $300-worth of human hair from Afro World Hair Company. Brownridge, who had worked as a painter for the company, said he planned lining his dog's kennel floor with the hair.

Officials in Rollingwood, Texas, have proposed a plan to spray-paint stray dogs so that their owners would call to complain, whereupon they would be charged with allowing their dogs to roam free.

NINE LIVES?

Critics have urged the US Defense Department to cancel its $2 million contract with Louisiana State University for research that involves shooting hundreds of cats in the head. The aim was to discover how to return brain-damaged soldiers to active duty, but so far the tests have indicated only that when a cat is shot in the head, it dies.

However, Cincinnati cats can breathe a little easier now that Professor Patricia Tornheim has called a halt to her 14-year research into trauma, during which she has crushed the skulls of 1,000 cats to test their brain reactions.

SNAKES ALIVE!
(AND SOME DEAD ONES)

In Philadelphia John F. Street introduced a bill to ban people from carrying snakes in public streets, parks and recreation areas. Street told the Philadelphia Inquirer the bill was needed because he was "tired of seeing people carrying snakes in public".

• •

In Quakertown, Pennsylvania, Gladys Diehl and her husband sued a mattress company and local department store, claiming that a 26-inch-long snake had been living inside the mattress they had bought. It was the couple's second such mattress; after they felt slithering in the first one, they exchanged it for another before they felt slithering in that one too. They took the second mattress to a testing laboratory, where the snake – by then dead – was discovered.

• •

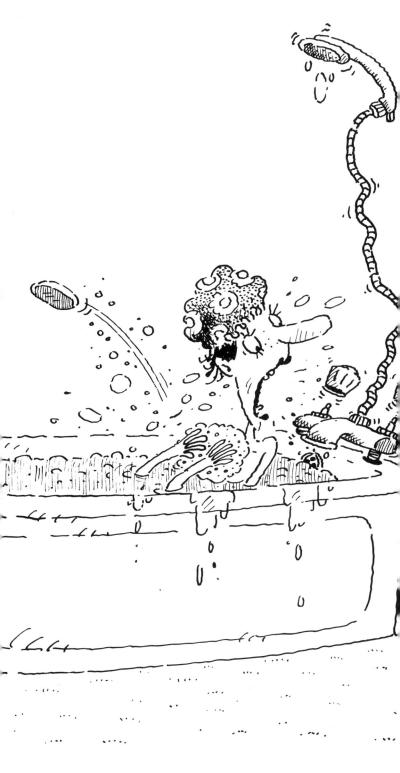

A man's body, fully clothed and intact except for some broken ribs, was found inside a 20-foot python caught in a village in central Sulawesi, Celebes.

Jason Ray Williams was sentenced to 90 days in jail in Houston, Texas, after pleading guilty to shoplifting a $150 ferret from a pet shop by putting the animal down his trousers and attempting to walk out with it. The arresting officer had frisked Williams a few weeks earlier and discovered a four-foot python wrapped round his leg.

Officials at the Houston Zoo admitted that their coral snake was a rubber imitation. "We had live snakes in the exhibit, but they didn't do well," said curator John Donaho. "They tend to die."

Florida Game and Fresh Water Fish Commission officials pulled a 74-inch boa constrictor out of Kathy and Ed Rogers' toilet in Coconut Creek after the snake had stuck its head out of the bowl for air while Kathy was in the bathroom.

HUNTERS HUNTED

In Pennsylvania Kelly Kyle, 17, was at home alone in the living room when she noticed deer in the garden. One suddenly crashed through the window and was followed by four others, after which all five proceeded to destroy the house. Kelly's father was out at the time – deer hunting.

A Virginia Beach man who was convicted of the second-degree murder of his mother-in-law told police he had mistaken her for a raccoon, while in Westchester a woman was shot when her husband mistook her for a woodchuck.

Whilst hunting in Kerryville, Texas, Hugh Day spotted a wild turkey. He climbed a tree and made gobbling noises to attract it, but so realistic was his imitation that another hunter shot him dead.

Gobble, gobble gob.

As a prank, two hunters in Adelaide, Australia, tied a stick of dynamite to a rabbit and lit the fuse, "just to see what would happen". What happened was that seconds before the explosion, the rabbit hid underneath the hunters' new truck.

It has been found that one of the leading causes of hunting injuries in the USA, totalling 36% of all cases, is not guns but hunters falling out of trees while sitting in wait for animals. Of 214 cases studied, 17 proved fatal.

A LOAD OF BULL...

For $4.95 Oregon Entremanure Enterprises of Salem, Massachusetts, sells greetings cards for you to send to people you don't like. Attached to each is a 10 ounce bag of cow, pig, horse, chicken and steer droppings.

• •

Animal rights activists urged sponsors of a Californian rodeo to cancel an event in which teams of three men wrestled with 500-pound steers. Once the animals had been knocked to the ground, the teams had to try to slip women's underwear on them.

• •

Among the activities at a recent conference of the American Zookeepers' Association was a contest for members to identify animal droppings in plastic bags. One contained a specimen the size of a coconut, which was instantly and correctly identified by all the contestants as having been produced by an elephant.

——— CHAPTER 5 ———

READ ALL ABOUT IT!

FIREMEN TO SHOW THEIR APPLIANCES T
PASSERS-BY TO ATTRACT ATTENTION
(Crawley Advertiser)

PRESS BOOBS & BLUNDERS

> Blackburn Times reporter Valerie will not forget the night she danced with Prime Minister Edward Heath at a Young Conservatives Ball – and ended up in the maternity ward of the local hospital.
> (*UK Press Gazette*)

"Even the dancing of go-go girls on such programmes as *Top of the Pops*, watched by millions of teenagers each week, leaves very little to the imagination," Mr Larkin added.
oooooo Judge H.C. Beaumont said.

(*Yorkshire Post*)

FEW HAVE ENTERED MISS CARMICHAEL

(Headline on the lack of support for a beauty contest in Carmichael, California)

Beginning in the winter of 1938, Dr Ewing and his associates, working on the deep-sea research vessel *Atlantis*, began to experiment with underwear photography. (*New York Times*)

'What I've Been Doing': Cecilia Bevan, mother of thirteen children. (*Radio Times*)

STRIP CLUB SHOCK – MAGISTRATES MAY ACT ON INDECENT SHOWS

(*Daily Mirror*)

• •

She has a fine, fair skin which, she admits ruefully, comes out in a mass of freckles at the first hint of sin.   (*Essex County Standard*)

• •

NUDIST NABBED: UNCLOTHED MAN, WHO ADMITS BRANDISHING PISTOL, IS CHARGED WITH CARRYING CONCEALED WEAPON

(*Providence Journal*)

• •

A Burnley man was remanded in custody for one week at Burnley Magistrates' Court charged with having sexual intercourse without consent. He was further charged with causing damage to a table.

(*Burnley Express*)

• •

The Duchesss smashed a bottle of champagne against the bow with unerring aim, and then, while the huge crowd cheered madly, she slid majestically down the greasy slipway into the sea.

(*Belfast News*, reporting the launch of aircraft carrier, *Bulwark*)

POLICE FOUND SAFE UNDER BLANKET
(Gloucester Echo)

BUS ON FIRE – PASSENGERS ALIGHT
(West Wales Guardian)

NEW HOME FOR OLD FOLKS IN THE PIPELINE
(Barbados Advocate)

MAN WITH SIX MONTHS TO LIVE JAILED FOR A YEAR
(Runcorn World)

MORTUARY TO BE BUILT DESPITE STIFF OPPOSITION
(New Malden Guardian)

FOOT SUFFERERS WILL GET A HELPING HAND
(Isle of Thanet Gazette, on a new mobile chiropody clinic)

999 MEN CHASE TWO BUSES
(Daily Herald, on police answering 999 call)

BRISTOL FLOWER GROUP PICK THEIR LEADER
(Bristol Evening Post)

CANNABIS SMUGGLING BY TROOPS. INVESTIGATION BY JOINT CHIEFS
(Morning Star)

The Ladies Literary Society will meet on Wednesday. Mrs Jones will sing *Put Me in My Little Wooden Bed* accompanied by the vicar.

(York Minster Choir Old Boys' Association newsletter.)

Mr George Dobbs of Chertsey is very proud of the fact that he walked 50 miles on a sausage sandwich at the weekend. (*Staines and Egham News*)

Two hundred and fifty pieces of Davenport porcelain, collected by a Lincolnshire woman over the last 20 years, will go under the hammer on February 12. (*Lincolnshire Echo*)

SMALL ADS

By popular demand the Tuesday afternoon club has become a coffee morning and in future will meet on Wednesdays.

(Aston Abbotts, Bucks, Parish magazine)

Give your wife a treat. Leave home this weekend.

(Advertisement by the Sun Inn, Kirkby Lonsdale, in the *Lytham St Anne's Express*)

1928 Rolls-Royce hearse. Original body.

(*The Times*)

Man of 38 wishes to meet woman of 30 owning tractor. Please enclose photograph of tractor.

(*Mountain Echo*, Himeville, South Africa)

Miss Goldhurst has no male goat this season, and refers all clients to Mr Harris.

(*Grantham Journal*)

For Sale: 100 year old brass bed. Perfect for antique lover. (London *Evening Star*)

**Head Thrower urgently required. A permanent
and well-paid position for the right applicant.
Coalport China Ltd.**

(Stoke-on-Trent *Evening Sentinel*)

TV NEWS

At 1:45 London Weekend brings you *University
Challenge*, followed at 2:15 by an in-depth leak
into the FA Cup - *look* into the FA Cup final.

(ITV announcer)

And there she is, the whole vast bulk of her.
(As the aircraft carrier, *Ark Royal*, was launched, Wynford
Vaughan-Thomas was describing the ship to BBC television
viewers – just as the camera switched to the Queen Mother)

Well, the streakers are at it again, this time at a
local football game just outside of Boston. I can't
figure out this type of behaviour – I guess it's
their way of showing they're nuts.

(Larry Glick, WBZ News, Boston, Massachusetts)

**I have just learned that we do
have the film of the astro-
nauts' breakfast, which
should be coming up shortly.**
(Frank McGee, NBC News, on
a Gemini space mission)

Pepper the parrot,
employed to speak in a TV
commercial for Alascom, a telephone company in
Alaska, sounded so human that he ended up
having his lines dubbed by a human actor imitat-
ing a parrot's voice.

In Palermo, Italy, 8-year-old Giusto Durante's
hands became mysteriously locked together after
watching Giucas Casella hypnotize someone on a
TV programme. Doctors tried to track down
Casella to get him to break the boy's trance by
telephone, eventually finding him in another
hospital where he was being treated after skew-
ering himself in the neck during a
mind-over-matter demonstration that had gone
disastrously wrong.

RADIO GA-GA

There is good news on the war front tonight. From North Africa comes word that Allied troops have stopped the advances of Hitler's Pansy Division. (BBC radio announcement, 1942)

As a joke, Dallas disc jockey Ron Chapman invited listeners to send him $20, promising "absolutely nothing" in return, but urging them to "beat the deadline". Within a couple of days he had received $240,000.

At Oxford Crown Court today, Donald Neilson denied being the Pink Panther.
(Edward Cole, BBC Radio 4 News, on the murderer known as the 'Black Panther')

The bowler's Holding, the batsman's Willey.
(Brian Johnston, commentary on 1976 Test, England *v* West Indies at the Oval, re: Michael Holding and Peter Willey)

GONE WITH THE WIND

When we were doing Personal Best, Robert [Towne, the director] encouraged us to burp and fart and swear a lot. He had been observing female athletes, and that's one of the things they do. I was great in the fart department.
(Mariel Hemingway)

And now, Whoopee John Wilfahrt and the Orchestra will play. (US radio announcer)

First of all Horizon on BBC2 tonight is doing a programme about the motorcycle, *Survival of the Fartest*. (Richard Baker)

Billie Jean King has always been conscious of wind on the centre court.
(Dan Maskell, Wimbledon commentary on BBC TV)

As you come over to join us, Ray Illingworth has just relieved himself at the Pavilion end.

(Brian Johnston, cricket commentary)

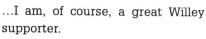

...I am, of course, a great Willey supporter.

(Trevor Bailey on cricketer Peter Willey)

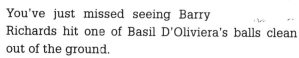

You've just missed seeing Barry Richards hit one of Basil D'Oliviera's balls clean out of the ground.

(Brian Johnston, cricket commentary)

Well, that's close of play here, with Hampshire 301 all out. But they go on playing till seven o'clock at Edgbaston, so over there now for some more balls from Rex Alston.

(Brian Johnston, cricket commentary)

SIGNS OF THE TIMES

Toilets out of Order. Please use Platforms 3–5, 16–20

(Notice at York Station)

Players picked for the darts team will be pinned to the notice board.

(Sign in Harehills Labour Club, Leeds)

Signal sent by destroyer to trawler: WHAT IS THE SIGNIFICANCE OF THAT SIGNAL YOU ARE FLYING?
Trawler to destroyer: REGRET I DO NOT KNOW. FLAGS SMELT OF FISH.

(Reported by Captain Jake Broome in *Make a Signal*)

—————— CHAPTER 6 ——————

LAST LAUGHS

ODD ENDS

A poodle named Cachi caused the deaths of three people in Buenos Aires. The dog fell from a 13th floor balcony and killed Maria Espina, by hitting her on the head. As the crowd gathered around Espina, an onlooker, Edith Sola, was knocked down by a bus and killed. Then a man who had witnessed both incidents had a heart attack and died in an ambulance on the way to hospital.

A young woman in Berkeley, California, was found dead inside her dishwasher. As the racks from the machine and her personal effects were stacked neatly beside it, police concluded that she had committed suicide.

In Palermo, Italy, the funeral of Antonio Percelli was halted when he climbed out of the coffin. His mother-in-law promptly died of a heart attack, and was later buried in Percelli's intended grave.

After singing several choruses of *Please Don't Talk About Me When I'm Gone* in a musical at the Moose Lodge, Towson, Maryland, Edith Webster collapsed and died.

After giving a speech to the Florida Toastmasters Club, on a visit to Johannesburg, in which he encouraged his audience to "Enjoy life while you can because death could strike at any moment," Danie du Toit, 49, collapsed and choked to death on a peppermint.

At Sherman's Amusement Park, Caroga Lake, 93-year-old Minnie Pearson was killed when her wheelchair hurtled off a roundabout.

After being gunned down in a Chicago motel car park, Willie M. Stokes Jr was buried in a coffin designed to resemble a Cadillac, complete with steering wheel, chrome radiator grille and flashing head and tail lights. Seated inside it, Stokes, 26, wore a red velvet suit and fedora and clutched wads of dollar bills in hands festooned with diamond rings. Spencer Leak of the A.R. Funeral Home described Mr Stokes as "Very car-conscious." As a

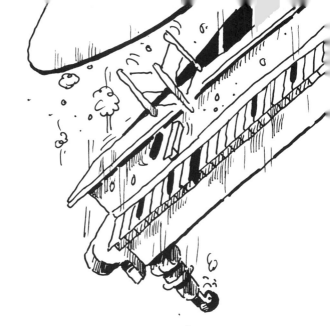

final touch, the coffin bore the personalized registration plate Stokes had used on his own Cadillac – 'WIMP'.

In Palatine, Illinois, Roger Ahalgrim has opened a 9-hole miniature golf course in the basement of his undertaker's parlour, together with a range of amusements that includes shuffleboard, ping pong, pool, video games and a haunted house exhibition with a guillotine, spider's webs, tombstones and coffins. The basement is used for birthday parties and other functions, but is closed when there is a wake in progress upstairs.

ASHES TO ASHES

A Hindu resident of Gympie, Queensland, had his deceased wife cremated, mixed her ashes in rum and drank it. "It was my way of showing how much I loved her," he explained.

WHERE THERE'S A WILL

A woman in Alton, Illinois, left her transvestite husband her entire $82,000 estate – excluding her dresses and accessories.

GRAND FINALE

In his will, John Cameron Young of Greenbrae, California, left $15,000 for a party to commemorate his life, with the specific stipulation that a piano should be dropped from a helicopter. He had often told his friend, Harry Murphy, of his dream: "He'd sit here and say, 'Harry – we've got to have a piano drop'."